For Mezi & The Saur,

The true inspirations in my life.

Contents

Introduction	3
WDYDWYDWYD?	6
What are your values?	8
What do you do to promote a learning environment?	10
What do you do to promote an innovation culture?	13
Are you aware of Parkinson's Law?	17
How well do you listen?	19
What is your purpose?	21
Epilogue	23
Acknowledgements	25

Introduction

For a number of years I have had a desire, a romantic dream if you may, of writing my very own book. The problem was that until recently, I had no idea what the purpose or the content of the book would be. Over the years I have tried and failed to think of a subject that I am passionate enough and knowledgeable enough to write about. That all changed after I challenged myself to give a keynote talk to my organisation.

I am passionate about learning and can often be found with earphones plugged in, listening to a podcast or a TED talk as I carry out tasks through the day. When not listening to audio information my head is often deeply buried in a book, trying to broaden and deepen my knowledge of the World that we live in.

It was one specific podcast (Noah Kagan's Coffee Challenge) that led me to challenge myself personally more than I would normally find comfortable to do. I don't believe myself to be a great presenter or talker, why would anyone want to listen to me waffle on and who the hell am I to be lecturing on subjects?

This was the limiting self-belief that I held for a very long time. So when the organisation that I work in began to have 'TED' style talks on Friday mornings, I saw this as an opportunity to challenge myself.

After a number of weeks discussing this with my colleagues, I forced myself to go into the organisers office and put my name down for the next available slot. I walked out of his office five minutes later having thought of a subject on the spot: *'What makes a good leader?'*

Shit! In an organisation full of alpha males, I instantly began to doubt myself. What shall I say? Who am I to say anything about leadership? What if nobody comes? What if people do come?

I let the wash of self-doubt settle, had a word with myself and began planning.

I decided on an approach of questioning rather than telling, I wanted the audience to question themselves, many of them who would be in positions of leadership, influence and authority. Seven questions relates not only to Military estimate planning but also to the suggestion that our brains can only take in 7 chunks of information, plus or minus two. So that gave me the basis of my plan, now to get some content.

The main objective of my keynote was to raise the awareness of leadership across all levels of the organisation. I wanted those in positions of authority to question what they are doing when leading and I wanted everyone, regardless of appointment to be conscious that anyone can be a leader, and just because they are not in a position of authority, doesn't mean that they aren't leaders.

But surely the military, especially a niche organisation such as mine, is abundant with good leaders I hear you ask? Let me tell you a little story to consolidate why I feel this talk was needed.

The details of the keynote subjects and presenters are published across the organisational intranet to encourage participation and attendance. The week leading up to my talk, I was chatting to a member of our organisation, who is in a senior leadership position and highly regarded within the organisation, whilst we made our coffee in the cafeteria. During our conversation, the person in question smugly asked; *'so, you are going to teach us how to be a good leader?'* I promptly informed him that the title of the talk was *'What makes a good leader?'*. His retort; *'same thing isn't it?'*, and quickly walked away. Now that is why we needed to have this talk in our organisation.

The following chapters are derived from the questions that I asked of the audience of my talk which was received better than I thought it would be.

Unfortunately, the individual with whom I had the conversation above with was not present, his loss.

I hope that you may get some value from the 7 questions that follow. Be honest and open with yourself.

WDYDWYDWYD?

What do you do when you do what you do? Take a moment and read it again, let it sink in, it's a bit of a mouthful I know. Now let us begin.

Are you aware of the environment around you when you do what you do? Do you understand that your actions and reactions do not occur in isolation? Too often we take our interactions for granted. We do not question what we do and the effect that it has upon the environment we are in. Sadly, critical reflection is not commonplace.

Self-awareness is a powerful skill that everyone should seek to develop further in their professional and personal lives. Self-awareness can be described as the conscious knowledge of one's character and feelings. Essentially if you are able to understand your own emotions, how they are unconsciously transmitted and how you react in times of communication, then you are in a far better position to understand the reaction of others during and following your interactions. As a leader, are you aware of the impact of your interactions?

A useful skill to enhance one's self-awareness is the concept of reflection in-action (Argyris & Schön, 1978) which is the ability to reflect on your actions whilst you are carrying them out. Through critical appreciation of your actions as they happen, you are in a better position to understand the effects of your actions; long and short-term, and able to consider whether they are best practice or require change to achieve the desired outcomes.

When brought together alongside experiential learning and reflection on-action, a term I am sure we are all aware of as it is fundamentally the way in which we learn from birth, a leader can evaluate in the moment and post event which can provide valuable insights for future action.

What are your values?

I don't mean the values that you are supposed to have because you are part of an organisation or that they are plastered all over the walls in your office or on the company intranet. If only it were so easy to instill values.

The values that I am interested in, and want you to consider, are you own personal ones. The ones that unconsciously drive everything that you do in your personal and professional lives. Have you ever thought about what they are and written them down?

For example, here are my own:

1. Personal mastery:
    a. 'Sweep the sheds' - adapted from the New Zealand All Blacks.
    b. Take responsibility for yourself, it is not down to anyone else.

2. Mana: adapted from Māori culture.
    a. It is honour.
    b. It is respect.

    c. It is power.

3. Excellence:

    a. Project it in all that you do.

    b. Expect it from others.

4. Purpose:

    a. Always question why!

You may notice that I have borrowed concepts from others, there is nothing wrong with that at all. That is often the way we learn, through observing others, iterating, and adopting what works and what we can relate to. The most important factor is that it means something to me, I relate to it and can hold myself accountable to it.

As a leader, do your values drive your leadership style or are they contradicting each other? Do you walk your talk and set an example for those around you? How do you measure yourself and hold yourself accountable?

What do you do to promote a learning environment?

The World is changing exponentially every single day and there appears to be no slowing down. The dawn of technology has created an environment of endless possibilities across all sectors and industries. Life as we knew it will never be the same.

Historically, organisations have relied on the age old tried and tested training delivery, to impart new knowledge and skills onto their people in reaction to a change in the environment. The main problem with this strategy is that it takes time. First of all you have to have noticed the change in the first place, then you need to understand what this change means to your organisation. The next step is usually to design and develop a training plan that will meet the new requirements, and then deliver the new material to your personnel.

By the time that this evolution is complete, the environment has changed again and you are reliving the entire process over and over just to try and remain current with the market. You can often end up in a reinforcing loop until something gives, which is seldom the environment. Not the most efficient way of doing things when you take this perspective.

Another way would be to empower the people you have in your organisation. What if all of your personnel were self-directed, self-motivated and self-actualising? What if you empowered your teams to use their initiative and be in a position to react quicker to changes in the environment or perhaps foresee then and get ahead of the curve. These are the principles of a learning organisation, which is underpinned by the principles of a coaching culture.

Is everyone within your team consciously aware of the organisational long-term vision and short-term goals? If not, then how are they best placed to make the decisions that matter in order to stay aligned to the strategic objectives? If there is no shared vision, then there cannot be a shared focus and energy will be lost as it will not be used effectively throughout the organisation.

How many within your organisation understand what systems thinking is? Of those that do, how many apply systems thinking in practice within the organisation? A system is considered a collection of entities, interrelated and interdependent which when bound together, act as a whole. Systems thinking is a way of viewing the World and all of its constituent parts, understanding complexity and appreciating messy situations.

An organisation is a system. Within it there may be many subsystems with the organisation itself possibly a subsystem of a larger system and so forth. Applying this holistic viewpoint, you can see how changes may affect different entities within the system itself, whilst also appreciating the impact upon entities outside the boundary of the system.

As a leader, what are you doing to empower those around you? What are you doing to ensure that your organisation not only survives, but thrives into the future?

What do you do to promote an innovation culture?

Organisations need to innovate, or die. Even more so in today's climate of continuous technological development. Human performance development is also catching up with the technology boom now. Many organisations are realising that the people within them are the greatest asset they have, and through their collective minds will create the future for the organisation.

So, where do you look to innovate within your organisation or team? More often than not, organisations like to create a neat little department and call it an "Innovation Hub" or some other ghastly modern equivalent in order to appear innovative. The problem with this method is that often, the people in that department are compartmented away from the remainder of the organisation so that they can let their creative juices flow. This usually has the opposite effect.. If people are penned in and encouraged to be creative, then it often becomes significantly harder to actually do the only thing that they are required to.

Instead of creating a singular department for innovation, why not allow the entire organisation the freedom to innovate? Encouraging all members of your team to be creative and take ownership for the future of the organisation can lead to astounding breakthroughs and perhaps the next big thing for your team to be successful.

Let me tell you a story;

Deep within the Amazon rainforest, there lives a small group of monkeys. The local tribe called them the "Macadamia monkeys" because of their love of the macadamia nut. The monkeys apparently go wild for the nuts and will do anything to get their hands on them.

The local tribe like to hunt the monkeys. They say their meat is the most succulent and full of flavour because of the nuts that they eat. The monkeys are clever little souls though and often hide in the tall trees within the forest to increase their chances of survival. The only problem with this is that the macadamia nuts fall to the floor of the forest and they have to go down to gather them all up so that they can feast on them. In doing so, they risk capture from the tribe and therefore have started to only go down to the forest floor during the hours of darkness.

Increasingly frustrated by the monkey's ingenuity to evade them, the local tribe formulated their own special plan in order to capture the monkeys. They use the golden coloured mud from around their camp to mould special pots. They shaped the pots specifically and secured a link chain to the bottom of them. The tribe then went out into the forest, where they knew the monkeys were, drove a stake through one end of the chain link to secure the pots to the ground before placing a handful of macadamia nuts inside and walking away from the area.

The trap was set. The monkeys, their senses far superior, could smell the nuts from a mile away. The smell was so strong it took all of their collective discipline to wait for nightfall before they descended the trees and went to harvest their food.

The tribe had laid in wait, far enough away as not to spook the monkeys but close enough to react to the inevitable. As the monkeys approached cautiously, the smell of the nuts became stringed, as did their desire for them. The monkeys slowly placed their hands inside the pots, collected the nuts in their hands and tried to pull them out. The problem was that the pots were not big enough for a fist to be removed. In an attempt to pull their closed fist out containing the nuts, the pots were raised off of the ground and yanked on the chains that were securing them to the floor. This noise alerted the waiting tribe that their traps had worked and they all started to close in on the trapped monkeys.

The monkeys were faced with a choice. The harder they pull, the more noise they made, but they could almost taste the nuts they were that close to getting what they wanted. They could see the safety of their homes high up in the trees and were aware of their enemy moving faster and faster towards them.

Their dilemma; to hold on to what they desire most at that time, or to let go and live to see another day.

Are you aware of Parkinson's Law?

The world will fill your time with problems unless you fill it with your own priorities. All too often in my organisation I overhear conversations where people will ask others how they are, and the reply is often 'busy'. This is sad, as 'busy' is not an emotion or a state of being, merely a perception of an environment. In a climate where everyone is 'busy', I want you to question if you are being effective?

The worst example of being 'busy' that I have experienced is from the people I will label the 'after hours emailers'. You know who you are!

There are very few exceptions where anyone should be sending emails out when everyone else has left the office. This does not show dedication, it conveys one of three things:

1. You are unable to manage your own workflow, unable to prioritise or delegate tasks and are overwhelmed hence you have to stay in work when others have left just to stay afloat.

2. You are ass kissing and trying to demonstrate that you are dedicated to the cause.

3. You have no life outside of work.

Neither of the above options are healthy for any individual and even worse for an organisation, especially if this is the behaviour from the leadership. This will inevitably filter down through the organisation and become the accepted culture which can have catastrophic long term effects on morale and health.

What impact does priority management have on yourself and those around you? As a leader, what example are you sending out to those around you regarding time and priority management? Are there always people sat around clock watching just because they feel they have to be in work? Or even worse, are they sat waiting for you to leave because it is unacceptable to leave before you?

The next time someone asks you how you are, I challenge you not you use the word 'busy'.

How well do you listen?

During a conversation with someone and whilst they are talking, do you find yourself already forming a response in your head before they have even finished? I'm sure many can relate as this is quite a common trait amongst many of us. Research suggests that only 10% of people actively listen.

Active listening is the most fundamental component of interpersonal communication skills. Active listening involves the use of all senses whilst giving all attention to the speaker.

Are you aware of the words being used, the tone, pitch and speed of what is being said? Do the words match the body language of the speaker, if not, why? Do you make eye contact with the speaker and are you aware of your own body language in relation to theirs?

It is too easy to prepare your answer in your head whilst they are talking, after all, your perspective is right isn't it? Or is it?

If you are guilty of the above, no need to worry. At least you are consciously aware of it now and can take measures to improve your listening techniques. Next time you are having a conversation, focus intently on not just what is being said, but the non-verbal communication that surrounds the words and often provides more insight than the words themselves. Try to take in as much information as possible and let the individual finish completely before giving your answer.

Before answering, consider asking them to clarify certain points of what they were saying to ensure that you have fully understood the context of their message. Take a mental note of how they react to your change of listening style.

The more we listen, the more we learn.

What is your purpose?

Why do you do what you do? Don't worry, we are not going to create another long abbreviation as we found in the first question but I do want you to take the time and really drill down into exactly what motivates you.

What is the real reason you get out of bed every morning and do the things that you do? Are your daily actions in congruence with your underlying purpose in life? If not, then you have to ask yourself why not? More importantly, you should consider making a change.

As a leader, how does your purpose affect what and how you do what you do? If you are a leader, is everyone aware of your purpose? If you don't share it with others, then how are they supposed to know what to do to assist you moving forward towards your vision?

Also if people are not aware, then how do they know if their purpose is aligned with yours? Too often, people with mis-aligned purposes, poor communication and all the good will in the World, will fail epicly and wonder why.

As a leader, figure out your real purpose, articulate it to those around you that matter, and then keep your purpose at the forefront of all that you do. Success will be waiting for you.

Epilogue

As a young soldier trying to learn his way through his chosen profession, I spent an abundant amount of time studying the art of war, leadership and great leaders of our time so that I may be able to learn something from them or perhaps emulate them.

A fundamental topic kept occurring through my research, to be a good leader one must be a good strategist. For too long, I held the impression that a great chess player was a great strategist and therefore an ideal leader. This led me to learn how to play chess, albeit poorly in a quest to become a good leader.

Whilst a grand chess master is clearly a great strategist, the leadership metaphor of a chess master would suggest that you have to individually move each piece around your battlefield. This strategy clearly has its limitations, specifically in the age we live in now.

A few years ago, I came across the metaphor that a great leader is comparable to a gardener. The gardener sows the seeds, provides the required nutrients and an environment that encourages the seeds to grow. The gardener's role is to maintain the environment, provide the nutrients required for growth, and allow nature to be nurtured.

This metaphor fits better with the modern day requirements of personnel who are self motivated, self-determined and self-actualising.

To that end, I implore you to go out and tend to your gardens with dedication and care.

Acknowledgements

I consider myself to be extremely fortunate to have lived a fulfilling and demanding life thus far. I have had the pleasure of working with an abundance of leaders, some who were in leadership roles and others who were not necessarily, but were still amazing leadership figures. There have been good leaders, bad leaders, immoral leaders, and indecisive leaders. I would like to express my sincerest gratitude to them all, I have learnt from each and every one of them. The lessons keep evolving too as I gather more experiences. Unfortunately, the list is too extensive to name people but I will always remember them and their lessons, implied or otherwise.

Thank you to you, if you are reading this then I appreciate the time you have given me. Time is our greatest asset so I am eternally grateful, and if I can be of help to you then please reach out to me.

Here are some of the sources of inspiration and concepts that have guided me along my personal developmental journey over the past couple of years;

Sheryl Sandberg - Her book 'Lean In' was inspirational in my own understanding of how I can assist in developing equality, specifically as a proud father to an amazing daughter.

Sir Richard Branson - 'Train people well enough so they can leave, treat them well enough so they don't want to'. His attitude goes to show that you don't have to be an ass to become successful in business.

Ricardo Semler - Ask three 'Whys?' in a row. The first time you have a good answer. The second time you struggle a bit, and by the third time you have no idea why you are doing what you are doing. I would encourage anyone within business to learn about the changes he implemented at SEMCO so many years ago. A visionary, way ahead of his time.

Tony Robbins - The epitome of a performance coach.

Simon Sinek - His book 'Start with Why' provides an enlightening approach to understanding the power of purpose that every leader should read.

Stan McChrystal - One of the greatest leaders of our times. His command and leadership styles within the military will undoubtedly shape the future of leadership development in both the commercial and government sectors.

Ryan Holliday - His book 'Ego is the enemy' has provided an explanation as to why people do certain things. Ego can be toxic in a leader, sadly I have witnessed the consequences and it is ugly!

Finally, I would like to express my heartfelt gratitude to the people closest to me who have given me ideas and support throughout the last 18 months since I had the idea of the talk. Without their help, none of this would have been possible;

Danny - The knowledge that at least one person would have been there at the talk was a weight lifted from my shoulders. Keep spreading the positivity that you do with every interaction you have.

Doc - Appreciate the barrage of messages that you have had to cope with over the past few years! All of your insights, advice and guidance have been fundamental to my own growth.

Keith - For always being available to talk and offer sound advice, and for making me feel that this was possible.

Noah Kagan - Appreciate your entertaining podcast and the fact that you reply to your own emails!

The Saur - my purpose. Her smile is all the fulfillment I need.

Mezi - The power behind all that I do. My partner in crime and the person who keeps me motivated and grounded all of the time. Thank you for being there for me all the time and giving me the energy to do something worthwhile.

Thank you!

For any further insights within the context of organisational development and human performance please visit www.quintessentialperformance.com or reach out on engage@quintessentialperformance.com, LinkedIn, Twitter and Facebook.

www.ingramcontent.com/pod-product-compliance
Lightning Source LLC
Chambersburg PA
CBHW070912220526
45466CB00005B/2195